Coloring book for adults and kids amazing ass image for design

This coloring book is belongs to

____

____

____

Back

www.ingramcontent.com/pod-product-compliance
Lightning Source LLC
Chambersburg PA
CBHW081243250726
48654CB00012B/1464